60 Second Leadership

52 lessons in personal and professional development for easy week by week application

Mike Greene

MANJUL
Manjul Publishing House

First published in India by

MANJUL

Manjul Publishing House

• 7/32, Ansari Road, Daryaganj, New Delhi 110 002
Website: www.manjulindia.com

Registered Office:
10, Nishat Colony, Bhopal 462 003 - India

Distribution Centres
Ahmedabad, Bengaluru, Bhopal, Kolkata, Chennai,
Hyderabad, Mumbai, New Delhi, Pune

Originally published by IntegrityWorks Coaching,
in the United States of America.

This edition first published in India in 2017

ISBN 978-81-8322-662-2

Printed and bound in India by Replika Press Private Limited.

This edition is authorised for sale in the following countries:
India, Bangladesh, Bhutan, Myanmar, Nepal, Pakistan and Sri Lanka

This book is dedicated to my wife of over 25 years, Amy. You are the quiet leader to whom I reference in Time Out 12. One of your favorite sayings is a verse in a country song, "Life's so sweet in the passenger seat". Happy to be in that seat, you quietly impart remarkable influence and wisdom in my personal and professional life. You are the rock and inspiration behind all I do. Every day, I'm inspired and incredibly grateful to come home to you!

Table of Contents

I don't need easy; I just need possible.

– Bethany Hamilton

Time Out 1
Goals Drive Performance

It was 1982. I was 16 years old and pursuing a goal. My dad and I got on the bus, and they drove us 26.2 miles away. We got out and headed to the start of the Philadelphia Marathon. My first. His, uh…probably somewhere around 60 or 61st. The gun went off and so did dad. I didn't see him for maybe half a day. So much for a nice father/son marathon experience. No matter. He had his goal; I had mine: to finish all 26.2 miles without stopping, and for a bonus – do it under 3 hours. Five miles in I bailed on the bonus.

At the halfway point, I was feeling pretty good, though that was somewhat relative because I had another 13.1 miles to go! Plus, I had some perspective. Two weeks earlier, as part of Coach Dad's training plan, I ran 20 miles of the Harrisburg Marathon. After 20 miles I practically crawled to my car and drove home.

Eighteen miles into this marathon, significant pain was enjoying a visit on the left side of my leg and hip. It's important now to remember that they drove us 26.2 miles out. Fact is, I had to get back, so running seemed most efficient, even with the pain. So I just kept pushing through. At 22 miles, I had no more pain. In fact, I don't remember feeling much at all. Not sure that was good, but I just kept going. At 24 miles, I knew I would finish, though not like I've seen others do it. No kick at the end for me – I was clearly on auto pilot. Nothing extra. Just finish. I was proud – 16 and completing my first marathon.

Then, I met her. Tabitha. I saw her name on signs all along the course. I even heard her name as I was running, but never really processed anything about it other than thinking it would be nice to hear and see my name occasionally. After all, Mike is a pretty common name. Just throw it out there!

Anyway, I had 60 and 70 year old men passing me in that last mile and it didn't matter. Why should Tabitha be any different? I'll tell you why. I'm now 47 and Tabitha is now 38. Quick math and you got it. Tabitha was a 7 year old girl. Passing me in the last mile. Remember that I said I had nothing left? Wrong. I just didn't have the proper incentive! That's right – pride kicked in and my revised goal was now to finish my marathon, not stopping, AND ahead of Tabitha! By the way, she had a brother running with her. He was 8 at the time. He didn't matter to me. It was all about Tabitha.

So as she passed I just inconspicuously let my foot drift out a bit and down she went. Goal accomplished. Kidding. As she passed I got motivated and found some energy I didn't know I had. I finished the race at 3:33:13. Tabitha finished at 3:33:16. Yep. Kicked her 7 year old butt! And her brother's too! So proud!

Frankly, Tabitha had no idea who I was or that I had a target on her back. Doubt she would have cared either. The point is this: my original goal drove me. It drove me to train right. It drove me to think right. It drove me to finish as planned. My new goal drove me to perform even more than planned.

What goals are driving your performance? Without them, you'll never do what could have been done. Find a goal that matters, that energizes you and chase it. Even if you fall short, you fall further, while learning and growing in the chase.

Hard work beats talent when
talent doesn't work hard.
- Unknown

Time Out 2
Got Heart?

I love watching Mitchell, our 15 year old son, play tennis.

A few weeks back he might have had the match of his career. Coaches generally say that if you just return the ball successfully 3 times, you'll almost always win the point. Yep – in most cases. Nope – not this time.

It was sunny, 80ish degrees, and they were playing their nemesis team. Mitchell was to play an 8 game set (first to 8 wins) in singles. He was matched against a common foe, though they have developed a healthy respect for each other over the years. Points were lasting far beyond the average 3 time return standard as the boys were committing very few unforced errors. And they weren't just returning; they were being aggressive, placing, spinning, charging the net – all of the above. They were both scrapping! I've played in rallies like this with Mitch, and it's very difficult to keep your form and footwork with that much energy being expended so quickly. And I'm a runner. These kids never gave in.

In fact, at one point, with Mitchell down in games 5-7 (his opponent needed one more game to win the match), a rally went for at least 40 or 50 shots – almost unheard of in tennis. It was eternal for us, the spectators; I cannot imagine how these boys felt! But, again, neither gave in. So impressive. Mitchell won the point and dropped on the court. He had forced his opponent to his far right with a strong forehand shot, then charged the net and closed the point with a winner to the opponent's far backhand. What none of us knew is that Mitchell had an asthma attack at the end of this rally. He told us later that he had 2 shots left, at best, and that's what prompted his aggressive closing shots at the end.

They eventually were tied at 7-7, leading to a tennis tie breaker. Mitchell high fived his opponent just prior to the tiebreaker, saying, "Are you ready for this, Noah?" and off they went. Well, I'm glad to say that Mitchell won the tie breaker 8-6 and consequently the match. It was remarkable to watch. An opponent's father came up to Mitchell after the match and said, "That was the best match I've seen in 3 years!" Amy asked Mitch who he was and he said, "I don't know, I don't care, but I like him!"

I share this because I'm probably a little proud… and because there were so many lessons these boys taught us from the court. The heart they displayed was the best I've seen all year, and maybe ever. They just did not give in – physically or mentally. They both showed great respect for each other – never disrespecting the game with poor attitudes, play call or effort. They even encouraged each other, commenting on great play as they went.

Heart. That's what they showed. They did their best, never gave in, managed their attitudes and emotions, showed mutual respect, and they were focused and poised, playing to the very end. They left it all on the court.

What if everyone was like that?

Treat people as though they were what they ought to be, and you will help them become what they are capable of becoming.

- Johan Wolfgang von Goethe

Time Out 3
Leaders Treat People into Existence

I can hear one of the most influential people in my life saying, "Mike, you'll lead far more effectively when you learn to treat people into existence."

Since the rest of the world generally focuses on what people do wrong, he told me to catch people doing things right. People move to where they feel valued. Rather than seeing people where they are, we would be better to see them where they can be – which supports what they value. That may take a little faith, encouragement and forethought, but it will prove well worth it.

Have you ever heard that capacity is a state of mind? Well, it certainly is, and others can significantly influence what we believe to be that capacity. Years ago, while in the role of selling for a local company (and with a locally competitive mindset), my manager/owner happened to mention that I was tracking at a nationally competitive level, of which I was completely unaware. Whether he knew it or not, his passive statement elevated me from being locally competitive to seeing myself as I could be – a nationally competitive sales leader (hit that a few years later).

If you want to develop a strong team at work, at church, on the field or at home – learn the patience and perspective of seeing people beyond their current state. Whether it's our spouse, our kids, or our team, people will generally rise to our level of expectation – especially with those who respect us most.

If you want a great team, treat people into existence.

The secret of your future is hidden in your daily routine.

- Mike Murdock

Time Out 4
Leaders Start by Guaranteeing a Win

I was talking to a friend and client the other day, and he was sharing about how his wife is up and running every morning – part of her daily exercise plan. He was acknowledging this to her and relating how he was impressed by her commitment. She said it's her way of ensuring a daily win.

I start my mornings with a guaranteed win by simply doing what I said I would do. Most of us fight that snooze button every working morning – perhaps because we're not inspired to get up and take on the day, or we're just tired and wanting more sleep, or we're just "conditioned" to snooze it for a few more minutes. Whatever the reason, I decided a few years ago that whether or not the snooze is a good or bad thing in my life is not the important issue; my self-discipline, or lack thereof, to get up on time, as planned…that is the issue. Who starts their day feeling lazy and expects to win?

So my day starts with a simple goal – 2 snoozes. That's it. I know when I need to be up the next morning and set the alarm to wake me 18 minutes ahead of that. (What's up with the 9 minute snooze default!!??) Anyway, I "allow" that bit of laziness, through snoozing, but manage it intentionally. As long as I honor the commitment I make – 2 snoozes – I am up on time and feeling good about my first "win". Then onto the next "win". I have several of these set up to start my day because, like my client's wife, I like to have those wins each morning as well.

Aristotle said, "The greatest victory is over self", and these wins are little, but powerful victories over self. They start things right. They start with us defining and following our own commitments. They help us earn a spot in the big leagues by developing one of the most powerful and common habits among winners – self-discipline.

Robert Schuller says, "Beginning is half done." So, nailing the beginning of our day…perhaps that puts us at least half way closer to the finish line of a highly successful day. Like the great Usain Bolt, and other top Olympic sprinters, getting a good start is paramount to the success of the race!

Let's get out of those blocks with some wins – some guaranteed victories – that we have complete control over. And then, as Dr. Laura says, we can "Go take on the day!"

Our chief want is someone who will inspire us to be what we know we could be.

- Ralph Waldo Emerson

Time Out 5
Influence Makes Me Sick

It was another beautiful morning. I got up, and with my wife, headed up for breakfast. Oh and it was good. Scrambled eggs, toast with butter, sausages, bacon – all that good, tasty, greasy breakfast food that makes the world a better place. And to top it off, we were sitting on a giant cruise ship, somewhere in the Pacific Northwest, on our way to Hubbard Bay, Alaska.

What I didn't realize is that the ship was getting into some nasty weather, and the power of influence was about to take its toll on me. We headed out of breakfast straight to the business meeting that we were attending that morning. We were seated in an auditorium area at one end of the ship. I was watching the guy on the stage as the curtains swayed, rather significantly, behind him. Now, I have a pretty strong stomach, but that influence thing started to wreak havoc on me as I watched people from the audience running out with their hands covering their mouths! I tried to tell myself, I feel fine; no problem here – It's just "mind over matter" – think good thoughts…all that stuff.

You know how it works, though. When you feel nauseous, your mind loves to mess with you by playing vivid images of your previous meal – the one still in your stomach, and perhaps wanting to leave, very quickly. Top that off with all the other people running out, with their hands over their mouths, kind of "convulsing" as they ran! I was doomed.

So, yes, I was sick, too. I was laying in the shower for a while, dry-heaving, while nearly half the ship was doing the same thing. My wife said nearly all the public rest rooms were closed – too messy to enter and too many to clean that fast. Just about everyone was in their cabins, the worst place to be. But, then again, who wants to be out in public, tossing their breakfast! The captain eventually aborted the Hubbard Bay destination, due to the bad weather, but we did ultimately go on to enjoy a wonderful Alaskan Cruise.

Was I really sick? Not sure. But the power of suggestion, the influence of those around me, coupled with the thoughts of a greasy breakfast, and that darn swaying curtain, did me in.

Influence is extremely powerful. We are influencing others, and they are influencing us. John Maxwell says, "Leadership is influence, nothing more, nothing less". While this illustration is a bit gross, it can be said that everyone influences, and, thereby, has some element of leadership responsibility.

How are you being influenced? And who are you influencing? Both are happening, all the time. As a leader in your workplace, your church, your community and your home – people are watching you – gaining permission to be lazy, take shortcuts, be impatient with others, and not follow through. Or they're being inspired to be tenacious, do things right, show patience and kindness to others, and always keep their word.

Who have you influenced this week? If they modeled your behavior, would you be proud or ashamed?

I think the answer we all want is obvious. Let's be more deliberate in getting it.

It's the little details that are vital.
Little things make big things happen.
- John Wooden

Time Out 6
Details and a Pool Table

In the DiSC profile, I am an "I-d" style. That means I prioritize results, action and enthusiasm. One of the common challenges associated with this style is the tendency to gloss over details. Hmmm…that's pretty darn accurate.

Over Thanksgiving break, my wife and I decided to buy our son a pool table for Christmas. We have a budget for our gift giving and we have three kids, so a typical pool table would not usually fall within budget. But Ebay has come through before…and it did once again. We saw a table that looked pretty good and at a remarkable price. So, while my kids and I were playing Monopoly, my wife was on the couch bidding on the pool table. As she won the bid, she just subtly looked over at me…we got it – for its original price – no one else bid against her. It was a steal.

Now the part I don't like. Details. Where is this table? How do we transport it? How do we lift it? How do we get it to our home without Mitchell knowing? How do we get it upstairs into his room? Details! We fire first, then see what comes next.

So, with that train of thought leading the way, I proceeded to gather up my daughter's boyfriend, borrow a minivan and make the 2 hour trip. This is, of course, without knowing the size of the table or the weight. Smart. But my mindset is always…we'll find a way. Nice optimistic perspective, but not always smart. By the way, the buyer did say something in the email about this being a really heavy table. No worries though – that's why we have two guys!

We showed up. The guy walked out, looked at all two of us, and said, "Ah…You're going to need eight guys." Not to be deterred, we spent an hour trying to figure out how to lift this (700+ pounds) table up the stairs out of the basement. The owner, by the way, was scheduled for hip surgery in a few weeks – no help was coming from him!

Needless to say, we left without the pool table.

Eventually, we did come back… with more guys. We did get it home. And it is upstairs, in his room. No damage to the table and, more important, no damage to any of us!

It was a lot more work than was necessary. Why? Because I glossed over the details. While I like my "we'll-make-it-work" attitude, I need to remember to be much more thoughtful in the beginning. We were pretty fortunate this time around – great table, fit in the van, did get it home – without damage and no one got hurt. Whew!

Next time I'll slow down and do it right up front. Probably.

The difference between average people and achieving people is their perception of and response to failure.

- John Maxwell

Time Out 7
Are You a PEAK Performer?

I heard a wise person years ago say that one form of hell is meeting the person you could have been.

PEAK performance is about closing the gap between who you are now and who you could or should be – as a business owner, salesperson, athlete, or anything that matters to you. First, is there a gap? Likely – yes. Second, what is your potential? Third, close that gap. Do it with a specific, intentional focus on becoming a PEAK performer. Here is my recommendation on becoming a PEAK performer in anything you want.

P means perspective. Perspective is about how you think. This is where it all starts. The couple going into their marriage with questionable commitment or an environment of disloyalty and disrespect comes in with the wrong perspective. It's a perspective prone to failure. That's the world they know – it's their current normal. This, of course, assumes they want a great marriage. To succeed, the mind needs a new normal. Get the right perspective. See things as you want them to be, not as they are. I believe perspective trumps all the rest. Give me a couple, a business owner, or an athlete with the right perspective – I'll bet on them first.

E means expertise. Expertise is about how you do what you do. How well do you do sales, business, marriage, parenting, exercise, etc? In baseball or tennis, it may be the mechanics of your swing. It's the intellectual part of the process – the "how to" of your objective. "How to's" become the pathways you build in your mind through proper execution and repetition. A great pianist didn't get that way by just showing up – they worked, they executed and they honed their craft.

A means action. Action asks the question "How often do you do what you do?" You can have great perspective (mindset) and great expertise (mechanics) but without ACTION it's just frustrating. You cannot steer a parked car. It may look good, but it ain't going anywhere! Getting consistent action out of my clients – especially sales related – is often my biggest challenge. How many times do you swing the bat? Are you executing enough to measure your mechanics, much less develop good mechanics? Just swing the bat, then begin adjusting and improving. As you read in John Maxwell's book, *Failing Forward*, quantity often produces quality – especially when properly coached.

K means knowledge. What do you know about what you are doing? Have you read a leadership book lately? As a business owner, do you understand enough about ROI, P&L statements, and fixed costs? Do you understand what makes your spouse tick, what motivates your kids and what energizes the individuals on your team? There are books and people that can help you in all these areas. Ask, be interested, engage and connect.

There you have it. Become a PEAK performer in the big rocks of your life – what's really important, but not always urgent. Start with Perspective – as Aristotle said, "The greatest victory is over self."

You are here to make a difference, to either improve the world or worsen it. And whether or not you consciously choose to, you will accomplish one or the other.

\- Richelle E. Goodrich

Time Out 8
People Math

Years ago our oldest daughter worked at a diner type restaurant. Toward the end of her stay, she encountered a bully. Her manager.

To give some perspective, it was her first job in this industry – a challenging one for sure. And her personality was timid at best, particularly in situations where she had little confidence. Two weeks prior to Easter, she gave her two week's notice – a gift to the employer – since being part time; a two week's notice is hardly common place. Anyway, she did, but a communication slip between when she told her supervisor (not the bully) and when the supervisor actually told the manager (the bully) ate into that two weeks timeline. Now, understand that she gave her notice in order to be done before the holiday so that she could join her family for a change. Her manager called her into her office and told her that she would have to work over Easter since she (the bully) was not told (by the supervisor) until that day – several days later. Remember, Britt tried to explain the communication mix up, but the bully would have none of it. I really think she liked the intimidation. Sick. When my wife picked her up, she was in tears. Good thing Amy didn't turn the car around and "meet up" with the manager! Amy is a very soft spoken, non-conflict type personality as well. Unless you mess with her kids. Might have liked seeing that! But she didn't. They came home and told the story to me. I'm not that big on confrontation either, but this is our daughter. I got on the phone and point blank asked the manager why she bullied Britt – a part-timer, who she knew was easily intimidated by her and was in tears in her office! After a few lame excuses and recognizing I was not a push over, she hung up. Nice. I called back. She took the call, and we'll stop there.

In life we come across adders, subtractors, dividers and multipliers. I call it people math.

Adders – add value to people; they enhance relationships and improve team performance by working with, not through, others.

Subtractors – only see negative; they point out what's wrong with you and the situation – actively and even worse, passively; they take away from every relationship – though it's usually not by intention – usually it's just their default. That's not an excuse, by the way. We all have the ability to become more aware of how we affect those around us.

Dividers – these people do what subtractors do, but they do it intentionally; they plan it – usually for their own self-serving purposes. They poison families, teams and cultures.

Multipliers – these people not only grow relationships, they grow others who in turn grow the team and relationships around them. Positive change and growth occurs through their influence even when they are not around.

What are you?

Care to guess where the bully falls in this list? Well, that was years ago, so let's hope the label has changed.

If you want small changes, work on your behavior; if you want quantum-leap change, work on your paradigms.

- Stephen R. Covey

Time Out 9
Own It

Words mean things.

I saw a commercial the other day and cringed at the choice of one word – "couldn't". The ad was about texting and driving and building another movement against it. No issue there. Heck, maybe we could even find an app that monitors car movement and zaps anyone who tries to text at the obvious wrong time! My issue is the choice of wording in one simple sentence, which says that people "couldn't" put their phone down. It may sound trite, but there is something wrong with our paradigm if we choose that word, or even hear it in that context, and miss its implication.

Couldn't. Or maybe better, wouldn't. Now that's more like it.

One suggests we are the victim. It's outside our control. How much success can we really have with things outside our control? It's a poor paradigm from which to change behavior.

The other suggests ownership. And thereby gives over control. How much success can we really have with things within our control? Tons! It's the right paradigm from which to change behavior.

Consider your words in the next few days. How many times do you choose words that divert ownership, give up control and leave you the victim? If we had the ability to record every word, then do a “find and replace”, I wonder how much positive change would occur? Here are two words I suggest we find and replace over the next 30 days – couldn’t vs wouldn’t and can’t vs won’t. Change the words, and you’ll begin to change your outcomes.

Keep in mind that our words precede our actions. We think. We say. We do. And then think again. Sometimes changing our thinking, while critically important, can be slippery. So perhaps the best way to influence behavior is to change our words – it’ll change our actions and eventually be a roundabout way to change our thinking.

Moving forward, let’s speak with ownership in our words. Speak like a victor, not a victim.

Every minute you spend in planning saves 10 minutes in execution; this gives you a 1,000 percent Return on Energy!

- Brian Tracy

Time Out 10
Prep and Landing

Fire! Just do it! Get moving! Make it happen!

Great mantras. And sometimes they really work. But often, they miss something very important. Proper preparation.

It was Christmas Eve and the sleigh was heading toward little Timmy's house to deliver his presents. Only problem was Wayne, the brooding, 227 year prep vet, who lost sight of his mission: Prep the house for Santa's arrival. As you may know, I'm referring to *Prep and Landing*, an endearing computer animated special introduced in 2009. The show isn't really about the power of preparation, but the point is clear. Without proper preparation, the mission is in danger and often will fail. Wayne's focus shifted from his mission – prep and landing – to his promotion, which he didn't get. Hence the brooding and lost focus during his mission. Fortunately, his goofy, rookie partner, Lanny, helped him get back on track, and Timmy got his presents, after all. Whew!

Proper preparation is key. For the high paced, hard chargers, it requires tremendous patience. For those on the other side – the detailed, do-it-right at all costs – this might be the quicksand that keeps us from taking our shot.

I've heard it said that luck is the place where opportunity and preparation meet. Sometimes, opportunity comes, and we are not prepared. Sometimes we are prepared and still don't jump at the opportunity. That's a different challenge…

I've struggled with this preparation thing most of my life. It does not come naturally, so I must be very deliberate to follow through. Scheduling time to plan and building the accountability to execute on that intention is a weekly effort for me – one I win much more now than in past years. The more I do it, the better I get. And, thanks to my wife, I have a prep rock star to help me along the way. Ask her about running out of gas in the middle of the night just over the Georgia border or about our drive to DC when we were first married. She left the preparation to me in those instances, and we have some very funny stories as a result! Though, they weren't all that funny at the time.

Preparation.

Are you ready for the next sales call? Are you ready for the upcoming coaching session? Are you prepared for the next proposal? Are you prepared for your next day, priorities in place, which, upon achievement, will have the greatest impact on your ultimate goal? Did you build a plan for a successful today and tomorrow?

You've heard it before, and you'll hear it again. Plan your work, then work your plan. Planning comes first. Then, it's time to execute.

Most people never run far enough on their first wind to find out they've got a second.

- William James

Time Out 11
Presentation Ain't as Important as Follow Through

You've all seen those great marriage proposals on YouTube, Facebook, and Pinterest. You know the ones – especially you guys. They are the proposals that are so crazy creative and romantic, they make us (lesser men) feel like putzes. I'm not even sure if that's really a word, but it just fits the feel. I once saw a guy sing to a girl on a cruise in front of the entire dinner audience and finish with a marriage proposal. All the women were completely gushing and all the guys just wanted out. Complete putzes. And the guy who proposed – not only did he have courage and a good voice, he was good looking, smart and confident. Hard to compete with that.

I've seen it in sales as well – the imaginative and memorable proposal that wows the potential buyer. The creative approach where they send one shoe to a prospect with a note that they'd love to get the "other foot" in the door. Imaginative, creative, different – all of those!

I don't know how those proposals work out in the long run. It would be interesting to find out. I do know that my marriage proposal was pretty lame compared to most of the ones I hear about. And as for my sales approach – I typically pick up the phone and call. Boring. Don't get me wrong – the passion and commitment are there; I just don't pull together all the props to wow the experience. What I do, though, is follow through.

My goal in my marriage is to be consistent in what I promised to Amy – that first day, at the altar. That's not to say creativity doesn't have its place. It surely does. But while I struggle with that right brain thinking at times, I make sure that I stay consistent in the small stuff in our marriage – opening the door for her, being truly "present" and engaged when I'm with her, and ultimately treating her the way she wants to be treated – the way that makes her feel best about herself and our marriage.

This works in sales as well. Feel free to wow the customer – yes. But never miss the small stuff – keeping in touch, adding value, following through on your word, being courteous and respectful.

If you're creative and you've given that remarkable proposal – great for you! Truly, I mean it. I just don't want to know about it! Meanwhile, make sure you stay consistent on the other stuff – that small stuff that adds up huge over time. That's the stuff that leads to deep honor, respect, loyalty. Love is a verb – an action – and it accumulates day by day.

Too many people overvalue what they are not and undervalue what they are.

- Malcolm Forbes

Time Out 12
Quiet Leadership

Are you a leader?

My wife (I'll call her Amy since that's her name) would definitely say she is not. But she would also be wrong.

Years ago Amy was in a homeschool co-op that included 40-50 families. They ran a regular school day once every two weeks at a local church. They would plan classes each fall and spring, set schedules, students and teachers, get lesson plans, monitor hallways, establish rules of conduct. They would plan and run kids plays, performances and other events. They would set up fundraising events, co-op funds, and expenses. They would promote the co-op and build membership in the co-op. They would establish leadership roles and responsibilities, meet as a team regularly.

When the director decided to step down, none of those on the leadership team really wanted to formerly step into that role, including Amy. So all four decided to share leadership evenly. Well, that type of plan rarely works as intended, and, as you likely guessed, Amy naturally rose to being the unofficial director. This wasn't because the others were incapable, but because their strengths were in other areas. As a team and individually, they would go to Amy for her final thoughts on things. When it came to vision and future thinking, it was usually Amy that stepped up, offered ideas, change and strategy. She never was named the director and would still say to this day that she was not the leader. From the outside looking in, she was. And everyone was good with it.

Hollywood tends to portray leaders as outgoing, driven, strong and decisive, hard chargers. And that is certainly true in many cases. Because that type of leader is so visible we may think that's all a leader is. I believe there are lots of leaders who don't see themselves as such, nor do they want to. They're the quiet leaders that aren't interested in the limelight or visibility of the traditional leader's role. Yet, their sense of responsibility, the level of respect they have with their peers and their vision will often "lead" them to the front, sometimes kicking and screaming.

Leadership is influence, as John Maxwell puts it. And influence is not limited to the outgoing, hard chargers. Influence is about respect – from those around us – however it's attained. That respect gets people's attention, and attention is where influence starts.

We are what we repeatedly do. Excellence, therefore, is not an act, but a habit."

- Aristotle

Time Out 13
The Language of Choice

One of the best teaching tools I've ever encountered helped me recognize that people behave in languages of communication far more elusive than what I was taught in English class. Being born in South Korea, I know only 4 Korean words; yet as I learned to understand behavior, it's not the words that really communicate the message anyway.

Oh sure, two completely different languages can be a huge barrier to effective communication; but let's be honest, most people who speak the same cultural language still experience huge barriers in their communication. We tend to speak and act on the basis of *our way* of communicating, rather than considering that others are attempting the same thing – but communicating in *their way*. And if we don't learn their ways, we'll miss them all day long.

Communication inefficiencies cost businesses billions each year, and cost families and marriages in far more ways than money can measure.

Stephen Covey nailed it in his bestselling book, *7 Habits of Highly Effective People*. Habit five says to "Seek first to understand, then to be understood". That is the foundation of great communication – getting our heart and head in the right perspective for effective communication – by seeking what the other person wants: understanding. Once we have that selfless mindset, we can use the tool of learning that has helped me so much in the past 25 years.

That tool is Everything DiSC®, and it helps to define the behavior styles of people by breaking them down into 8 blended styles of communication. Those styles vary from blends of 4 keys points of behavior and various levels of inclination in each style. To keep it simple, the four styles include:

1. The D – Dominant (fast-paced & outspoken/questioning & skeptical)
2. The i – Influence (fast-paced & outspoken/accepting & warm)
3. The S – Steadiness (accepting & warm/cautious & reflective)
4. The C – Conscientious (questioning & skeptical/cautious & reflective).

Different words will resonate with each style. Can you classify which of the following words describes which style, or more important define your spouse's style, your co-worker's style, your client's style, or your child's style? – Challenge, Drive, Action, Encouragement, Collaboration, Support, Reliability and Objectivity. What drives their behavior? Knowing can be a difference maker.

I encourage you to learn more, understand more, and apply more in this area of communication. Many of you reading this have heard of DiSC or MBTI, or many other methods of behavior assessments, yet the vast majority spent a few minutes reading their personal results and then did what most of us do with new learning. We put it in a drawer, or file, never to be visited again. Knowledge unapplied.

Take it two steps further this time: Get the knowledge, yes; but then, take it out and apply it, then keep applying it – consistently. Over time it will be a learned behavior, and, with the proper mindset of seeking first to understand, you'll be invaluable in your relationships – at work and at home.

That's something worth becoming.

Most people do not listen with the intent to understand; they listen with the intent to reply.

- Paul J. Meyer

Time Out 14
Stop Talking!

At the end of a workshop the speaker was asked a quick question. Well aware the session was all but over, he allowed this one last question, and then proceeded with his response. Interestingly, the speaker seemed aware of the time situation, even alluding to it with comments like "wrapping up soon." But he just kept on talking. I think the speaker really thought what was being said took priority over honoring the time – OUR time. I believe the speaker was the only one in the room that felt that way.

Bottom line, and I see it more and more, is this: People talk too much!! And on top of that they ask very little. And when they do ask, it's usually a set up for them to talk more!

I am speaking of people in both professional and personal settings. I am shocked at the amount of uninvited information or over expanded detail that is offered in conversation – even sales conversations – and professional sales people should absolutely know the difference.

In fact, I just ran into an old acquaintance recently. We spoke for about 15 minutes, and he asked exactly zero questions! None. Am I that uninteresting? Don't answer that! But, seriously, I was probably very interesting to him because I let him talk, and talk, and talk. And he liked talking. But was he interesting to me? Not at all.

So, here are a few ideas. One: Don't assume you're so super interesting that you can overcome throwing up big chunks on people and still come out on top. Two: Listen with your eyes while you talk – be aware of their interest level and finish well before they glaze over. In other words, leave people wanting more, not wanting out! Last: Ask questions. Get others talking about themselves. Learn from them. The person who is talking cannot be listening.

Be the listener, not the talker. The listener is the one who shows value. And people move to where they feel valued.

Never doubt that a small group of committed citizens can change the world; indeed, it is the only thing that ever has.

\- Margaret Mead

Time Out 15
Don't be the Magic

Being the magic, isn't it awesome? When things really need to get done, you step in as the one person who can and will make it happen. Just like Moses, as he led the Israelites through the desert, and, ultimately to the Promised Land. Sounds good on the surface or in the beginning. But the problem with being the magic is that when you leave, the magic leaves. The magician is a prisoner of his own talent. Not necessarily a good thing.

As you read through the chapter of Exodus, you'll find Moses was the magic until a very wise Jethro set him straight. Jethro was Moses' father-in-law. He witnessed the people of Israel bringing all their issues and disputes before Moses, who would bring judgment in these matters. He would be fully engaged from "morning until evening" just to be judge over all the people – and there was a lot of them!

Jethro recognized that this was not sustainable by one person and told Moses to equip leaders within the Israelite community who would learn to listen, teach, and judge, much like Moses. In time, these leaders would be chosen to manage the affairs of the people, and only bring the most difficult of circumstances before Moses.

Jethro taught Moses that he could not effectively be the magic, certainly not in the long run. He needed to spread the magic – by teaching and equipping other leaders. It became one leader, developing leaders who led leaders to lead. Spreading the magic, not being the magic. That's leadership!

Quite honestly, many of us like being the magic. Or we simply don't trust others being the magic. It's a failing leadership philosophy either way. None of us will ever be as good as all of us. Well equipped people can accomplish far more than one very exhausted magician.

I've learned that people will forget what you said, people will forget what you did, but people will never forget how you made them feel.

- Maya Angelou

Time Out 16
Stop with the Pronouns!

They are weak.

They are uncaring.

They are impersonal.

They are pronouns.

I must first say that I have never seen anything written on this…which might say something. But, I firmly believe there is tremendous value in the little example I'll share in the next few paragraphs. And, by the way, I correct myself; I have heard my wife share the same opinion on pronouns. And that's all the backing I need.

Think about your last leadership team interaction. Your managers were there with you. And you were talking, leading, strategizing. Whatever. When you came to a point of indirectly referencing one of your leaders, did you do so by name or did you use a pronoun? Stay with me here. This is important, whether they even notice or not. Because we do, at some level. We all notice the difference. In the following simple examples, let's assume everyone is present.

Take **him** with you on the next call. Rather, take **John** with you on the next call.

You're going to need those reports from **her** as soon as possible. Rather, you're going to need those reports from **Jane** as soon as possible.

She's going to offer her ideas, then… Rather, **Anne's** going to offer her ideas, then…

Don't discount this. I know of several leaders who make this mistake often. And I know they care. But their words don't tell a caring story at times.

Research has consistently shown that a person's own name is the single most important word to him/her. Our name is intimately tied to our identity and value as a human being. Whether or not you use a person's name, and how you use it, has a profound effect on their impressions of you.

Names matter.

When it comes to those close to you – your family, your team, your friends – keep it personal, by NAME.

Don't let yesterday take up too much of today.

- Will Rogers

Time Out 17
Take a Step Back

Sometimes you just have to step back. And then be thankful with what you see.

Most of the time we see our kids, our marriage, our jobs, and our life from just inches away. You know when you're that close, you see everything *wrong*. Every flaw, every goof, everything that's out of place, misguided, the stress lines and struggle – it's magnified by our *choice* of perspective.

When you look at your car after a much needed wash or look at your house with the new Christmas lights now up, where do you stand? Do you stand right there in front or do you step back – far enough to really get the right perspective?

It's time to do that with what really matters. Step back and really look at your kids. My wife and I will do this occasionally – and yet not enough. We'll get frustrated, just like every other parent, with the poor decisions, laziness, disrespect, etc. But ultimately, when we step back and look at the "masterpiece" we are constantly working on – our children – we really do like what we see. They're pretty good kids, despite those flaws. Flaws that we happen to have as well. And Amy and I don't really believe we're the true architects anyway. We're just facilitators in a grand scheme. The question is what are we facilitating? By focusing too closely, our attention is in the wrong place, and we'll tend to highlight what's wrong. If we step back, we get the right perspective and tend to promote what's right. You get the idea.

How do you step back? Well, you choose for one thing – be aware and decide, often. Another way is by changing your environment. Find a great getaway for you and the kids. A place where you can see each other out of life's typical routine, where you can connect and reflect. I just met with a friend who spoke of this. They have a getaway in a remote part of the state. His wife wanted it and he didn't – said they'd never go and yet years later he's reflecting on how thankful he is to have yielded to her wisdom. It's a tradition for their family that promotes perspective – the right perspective. We've been doing the same thing with our family by spending a week in WV every fall – for the past 14 years. Our kids even cherish this time and place more than any other getaway – including the beach!

If a getaway isn't an option at the moment, Calgon suggests taking a bath. Maybe start there.

As you step back, be thankful. That one day a year when we tend to collectively think in terms of a grateful, thankful heart, will be here before we know it. Try being bitter and thankful at the same time. Doesn't work. One wins out. You choose. I choose thankful, and I make it easier when I step back.

No one has ever become poor by giving.
- Anne Frank

Time Out 18
Takers, Traders and Investors

Years ago I heard a highly successful businessman tell a story about his leadership journey and how one statement from his dad completely changed his success pathway. This man was in business with his dad, building an organization of leaders for personal and professional development. They would hold meetings at regular intervals to share their business idea with potential leaders who might join their mission. He would only attend those meetings when he had something personal to gain – like growing his organization by those he invited. If he had no one personally attending, he would no show. Eventually his dad pulled him aside and simply told him, "You are a taker". How would you like to hear that from your dad, particularly if you're part of his business?

In a recent audio I heard the speaker share something similar, but broke it out further. He said people tended to fall into three categories:

1. **Takers** – These people do what the label says and what the man referenced above was doing – they take. They do not give. They show up to receive. They speak to be heard. It's about them and them alone.

2. **Traders** – These people give *conditionally*. Traders try to

fool us and sometimes themselves. They will help, but only if it will be reciprocated. Some are outright about it; others just keep score and, trust me, payment will be required – eventually. Interestingly, I'd prefer a taker over a trader. At least takers are clear about their interest.

3. **Investors** – These people give, and often receive; they just don't plan or make *receiving* the condition. In a way, the lack of return is a gift in itself. They're investing in the relationship, the cause, the opportunity. The mere definition suggests there will be a return, but that return is not guaranteed, nor is the level of return. These are the unconditional, unselfish leaders you want in your organization and your life. The best marriages are built with investors. The best businesses are made up of investors. The best teams thrive with investors.

This year, let's commit to being investors. Let's give. And give again. Let's invest in people, even ourselves. Let's invest in our marriage, our kids, our teams, our community, our church. Let's not keep score.

After hearing Anne Beiler of Auntie Anne's Pretzels speak at a local leadership event, I remember one thing that stuck with me. Here is what she said, "Give, to get, to give again". Pretty much nails the investor mindset.

Progress is impossible without change,
and those who cannot change their
minds cannot change anything.
- George Bernard Shaw

Time Out 19
The Comfort of Change

If change is comfortable, you're doing it wrong.

As you've already read, my son Mitchell is a tennis player. He loves it. He's also extremely coachable, as long as it's not his dad doing the coaching. Truth be told, the best coaching at this point comes from him to me anyway.

One day he was helping me with my serve – working on grip, position, feet, movement, ball toss, and leverage – just a few little things to consider ALL AT ONCE! When we really started adjusting my serve, the grip he showed me was awkward, and I complained in my best subtle fashion. You know how to do it, too – you complain with a smile – that way it seems like you're kidding, yet you've managed to get it on record that you don't like it! Well, when I offered up my subtle whining, he provided some pretty good advice. This 14 year old profoundly said to me, "Dad, if the change is comfortable, then you're doing it wrong."

Wow! That hit home, though I can't say I haven't been silently arguing over the past few weeks. I'm 47. Why do I care about the "perfect" serve anyway? Here's why I care – if for no other reason, submitting to proper teaching is a much better example for my son!

Regardless of my personal struggle with change on the tennis court, the advice is dead on accurate. How much change do we take on, only to adjust it to a more "comfortable" level? When we do this, we rob ourselves of the real rewards that come from correct and consistent change.

Do you want a better tennis game? How about a raise? Do you want a better, more rewarding career? Do you want a better marriage, better relationships with key people in your life?

Change. Don't adjust to your level of comfort; keep it consistent with proper coaching and the ultimate reward you want.

By the way, my serve is starting to improve. Major headway on the court yesterday. Thanks, buddy.

And in the end it is not the years in your life that count, it's the life in your years.

- Abraham Lincoln

Time Out 20
The Crazy Cycle

What he said made absolute sense. He was tired, out of shape and stressed. And when you're feeling that way, exercise is obsolete and eating poorly is easy because, well, it's easy. So, more convenience eating and less real exercise leads to wider hips, a bigger belly, slower metabolism, less energy and more stress. What's the mathematical principle? Two negatives added together equals a negative. That's the crazy cycle.

At some point, the crazy cycle needed to be turned around. And it was.

In high school I became addicted. That's right, I had an addiction. It was running. I got to the point that running daily was like brushing my teeth. It was just something I did. A real habit. Eating, on the other hand, was not stellar, but it didn't matter then. Being 16 with high metabolism, I could get away with it.

This man is not in high school anymore. He's married, has kids and a very demanding job...you know the equation. Most of us live it. And if we're not careful, all of those reasons can become excellent excuses to stay in the crazy cycle. I say reasons because that's what they should be. To the extent that we can influence our physical and mental condition, our families, friends and careers are good reasons to be healthy. Aren't they? To me the goal is not just living; it's living with vitality, energy and passion, with more to give to those we love – now and long term.

So let's go there – it's the energizing cycle.

Back to my friend. Here's something I knew about him: he'll meet a challenge if he truly commits to it and respects the person to whom he's accountable. It's how he's wired. His integrity – say what you mean, mean what you say – rules his decisions. He committed to me and said he'd do the same with his wife – to exercise 3 times a week for a minimum of 15 minutes. And he decided to start that day. And he did.

What he'll eventually experience, I hope, is the energizing cycle. When you exercise consistently, you'll want to eat better. And when you eat better, you'll significantly jump-start the effects of your exercise – you'll look and feel much better, inside and out. And when you look and feel better, you want to keep it that way, so you… You get the picture. The energizing cycle.

In case you're wondering, my friend is several weeks in now and continues to be true to his word. He chose to be accountable, and his integrity is stronger than his temporary emotion. He sees how he can, not why he can't. And soon, he won't need the accountability because when the energizing cycle hits, he'll naturally feed his own motivation.

What's the mathematical principle? Two positives added together equals a positive.

Go for the energizing cycle. It's a fabulous ride!

Men are anxious to improve their circumstances, but are unwilling to improve themselves; they therefore remain bound.

- James Allen

Time Out 21
Who, Where, Why

It's a terrible blizzard in the dead of winter. The woman was frazzled, to say the least, as she followed behind the huge snow plow. It's what her father would do, she told herself. So she followed, closely and carefully. Suddenly the big plow stopped. The driver got out, walked over and tapped on her window. She opened the window, and he asked why she was following him. She explained that her father always told her to find a snow plow and follow it if she was ever caught in a blizzard. The driver grunted, and as he walked away said, "Well, alright, I've finished the Walmart lot. Let's head over to K-Mart next".

We're all following someone. The obvious question might be who? But the bigger question is where? A friend many years ago used to say that our income was the average income of the top 5 most influential people in our lives. I never really checked the validity of that statement, but I sure get the context. It likely applies across the board – to our habits – which in turn, impact all the other areas of our lives. Whoever those influencers are in our life, check their habits and their results against the most important parts of your life and ask the question "Do they have what I want where it matters most, or are they at least headed in that direction, perhaps a little further down the road than me?" That's a great question.

Are you in sales? What level of success do you want? Who's influencing you most? Are you deliberate in that choice? Are you married? What type of marriage do you want? Who's influencing you and your spouse most? Are you a business owner? You get the idea.

And keep in mind that our top influencers may not be through direct personal relationships. We are influenced by all areas of input – including TV shows, radio, internet, and books – everything we are exposed to.

As a trainer and coach my goal with clients, especially in coaching, is less about teaching and more about influencing. I want to inspire positive, behavioral change based on the outcomes desired. And that is best done slowly, consistently and congruently.

Following the snow plow was safe. But where did it get her?

So I ask again: Who are you following, and where are you going?

When you do the things you need to do when you need to do them, the day will come when you can do the things you want to do when you want to do them.

- Zig Ziglar

Time Out 22
The One Thing

Unlimited membership, yet limited space. That's right – any gym in January! Good people with good intentions and plenty of motivation, yet so few who are still showing up in March. And there, too, go their goals! Let's look at one common reason…

Typically, when we are ready to commit to change, we want to commit to *too much change* – which usually yields no change at all! Brian Tracy, world renowned motivational speaker and author, advises that we choose the ONE THING that if done effectively and consistently over the next 90 days would have the greatest impact on our desired outcome. What do you want? Then, what should you be doing (the one thing) to get it?

How about your job? What one thing, that if done effectively and consistently over the next 90 days, would have the greatest positive impact on your job performance? How about your marriage? What one thing, that if done effectively and consistently over the next 90 days, would have the greatest positive impact on your marriage? What about health and fitness? What one thing, that if done effectively and consistently over the next 90 days, would have the greatest positive impact on your health? You see, there are **so many things** we could do to improve our job performance, our marriage or our health. Trying to tackle all or most of them? How's that been working?

Let's clear the screen, and put the blinders on, and imagine that only ONE THING really mattered. Let's also be honest – if you focus on that ONE THING, other stuff will still get done. The key is that the action that provides the greatest return is fully leveraged, with consistency and very specific intent. That will provide the greatest return on effort!

Let's go – if you could only make one change, what would you change? Decide, execute for 90 days – finish what you start – then and only then look back.

The world is full of great starters. It's the finishers that are the ones to watch.

Success is not final. Failure is not fatal. It is the courage to continue that counts.

- Winston Churchill

Time Out 23
The Principle and the Lighthouse

This is the transcript of an actual radio conversation between a US naval ship and Canadian authorities off the coast of Newfoundland in October 1995. The Radio conversation was released by the Chief of Naval Operations on Oct. 10, 1995.

US Ship: Please divert your course 0.5 degrees to the south to avoid a collision.

CND reply: Recommend you divert your course 15 degrees to the South to avoid a collision.

US Ship: This is the Captain of a US Navy Ship. I say again, divert your course.

CND reply: No. I say again, you divert YOUR course!

US Ship: THIS IS THE BATTLESHIP USS MISSOURI; WE ARE A LARGE WARSHIP OF THE US NAVY. DIVERT YOUR COURSE NOW!!

CND reply: This is a lighthouse. Your call.

This is not actually a true story, but has been circulated as such for many years. I've heard it and you've likely heard it as well. Yet, take a moment to really consider the point beyond the obvious humor. Techniques can change but principles never do. They're steadfast.

I've done sales training for many years now. The most common questions I get are about technique – how to close, how to approach, what to say, how to ask great questions and drill down, how to gain agreement, how to mirror, on and on. All good stuff. Except, if it's done outside of principle it's often not very effective. At least not for long term client relationships.

What's principle? It's the "why" behind the process. It's knowing why you're asking questions, why you're drilling down, why you're gaining agreement, why you're trial closing, why you're mirroring and on and on. They're the lighthouses; they don't change. They're unmoving, resolute. In fact, if you know the why – and you don't give up – you'll figure out the how.

Technique does matter. It sure makes the process smoother and often quicker. So don't discount it – get it, learn it, own it. But it has to be built on solid principle. I'll take a person who gets the principles of selling before I consider the one that just has great technique. Given one or the other, I'll take principle every time. I can build on that.

But give me both – technique built on strong principle. Now that's a winning combination.

A man is about as happy as he makes up his mind to be.

- Abraham Lincoln

Time Out 24
Unhappiness Comes From Comparison

"Unhappiness comes from comparison". This is a statement a long time friend uttered many years ago – and one that has stuck with me ever since.

Think about it. We do this all the time. We compare houses, incomes, jobs, sports prowess, bench press, kids, spouses, cars, jewelry, clothing, churches, and on and on. And probably more often than anything else, we compare situations, perceived circumstances and conditions of others. I would like to say I'm not that petty, but I know subconsciously, if not consciously on occasion, I find myself comparing some of those things – particularly situations. Some comparison can be helpful, if managed in a competitive and productive way, but that's not what I'm speaking about here.

I remember a well known preacher saying that sometimes we see a preacher in the "zone", connecting beautifully with passion, purpose and charisma. What we see at that moment is them at the top of their game. Once they step away from that pulpit it's usually downhill, perhaps not in a bad way, but it's just not as good – no one stays in that zone, consistently. But in the world of comparison we tend to take that person's best and attribute it to everything they do – as if they are in the zone in all things, and at all times. And then we compare. With that, we don't have a chance.

I remember hearing another person say that the devil loves to get us comparing some else's best to our worst – a pretty unfair fight. But then again, that kind fits that guy's plan.

If it's true that all or much unhappiness comes from comparison, then maybe the real lesson lies in applying the opposite perspective. Happiness comes from within. No outside comparison, just plain old internal perspective. It may still be inspired by outside conditions, but ultimately it's an inside decision. Many times I see people with seemingly similar circumstances, yet completely different perspectives – an inside decision.

Wow, I'm learning as I write this. Maybe that's why I'm writing it. Hope it's helpful to you – as happy people are statistically more productive in all things – careers, health, relationships – all that matters. So I guess it's our choice, happiness. What do you choose?

You cannot truly listen to anyone and do anything else at the same time.

- M. Scott Peck

Time Out 25
Silence Speaks

Ever try to stare down a dog? Not a challenge as, eventually, she'll get distracted or bored with looking at you. Ever try that with a cat? If you did, you may still be doing it because the cat doesn't look away. They're tough to stare down. It's almost creepy. I think they know the one who looks away is the one NOT in control.

Years ago I had a manager who had a very unique style of communication that was exemplified in certain strategic situations. I often tell this story as it teaches some great lessons. We would meet in his office to discuss ideas, strategy, sales, or simply something I wanted. Upon my presentation of ideas, I would pause, as is the common protocol of communication (Ok, I'm done, your turn…). Then it got interesting. He would simply look at me (felt like the cat stare) and…nothing. After an eternal 3 second pause, I'd start talking. He obviously needed more. And then I would stop – remember, his turn now. Another stare, pause. And, you guessed it, I'd start talking again. And so it would go. Inevitably I'd leave the meeting having not gained what I wanted or feeling like I lost credibility or whatever I thought I had coming in.

After several of these engagements, I decided to change my approach.

I walked into his office, sat down, shared my thoughts…then, I shut up! He stared. I stared. He continued staring. I began sweating (in a Cool Hand Luke sort of way, of course), but continued staring. This is absolutely true! Finally, after 30 minutes (probably more like 20 seconds, but it felt like half an hour!), he spoke. And guess what? I usually walked out with my ideas accepted, more confidence and ultimately more influence. Did I stare him down? No – what I did was mirror his communication. Even though it was, and still would be, very uncomfortable for me, I adapted to his style and gained better communication and influence because of it. Was he staring me down? No – he was thinking, which translated into focus and silence. And guys like me don't really understand silence – we tend to think we must fill it, usually with us. Usually not good.

Ultimately, I believe the relationship was far more effective when I learned to communicate in a style that worked for him, and me. Let me also say, this is a wonderful individual, for whom I have great respect. His communication was just different than mine, and I learned to recognize and embrace it.

I did and we succeeded.

Thunder is good, thunder is impressive; but it is the lightening that does the work.

- Mark Twain

Time Out 26
Dialogue of the Deaf

I don't really know what an argument would look like between two deaf individuals, but I have seen plenty of conversations that almost looked as if both people were deaf. You've seen it. They talk, but no one listens. They try to make THEIR point, and yet they're building that very point at the same time the other person is trying to make theirs! How much listening is involved? None!

By no means do I mean any disrespect to anyone who is deaf. I suspect that anyone who is deaf would find it sad and ridiculous to see two people with perfectly good hearing acting like they can't really hear each other – by choice.

I read in *The Significance Principle*, by Les Carter and Jim Underwood, that we should listen PAST where the other person has finished. We should even pause before answering. This doesn't just apply to a "heated" conversation, but any conversation. Let them talk! Let them get their point, their story, their compliment, and even their criticism out. Completely. Then, before preparing your response, ask more about what they said. Get engaged. Understand what and why. Stephen Covey defines this as the 5th habit in his top 2 selling business book of the 20th century, *7 Habits of Highly*

Effective People. It's critical: Seek First to Understand, Then to be Understood.

Seeking real understanding affirms the other person and what they have to say. That's what they want. That's what we want – to be understood, valued and affirmed.

What if you seek to understand, but others don't? Two things come to mind. One person truly listening is generally better than none. More important though, one person listening generally leads to two people listening. Others learn the habit through your example. It's your influence, and as John Maxwell says, "Leadership is influence, nothing more, nothing less".

Do you want to be a better leader? Avoid the collective monologue. Think; don't react. Allow stimulus of another's words to yield CHOICE which then yields response. Choice, in this case, is your decision to listen, pause, consider, engage and then respond to others. Try it. It works.

It's not what you do once in a while; it's what you do day in and day out that makes the difference.

- Jenny Craig

Time Out 27
Easy to do Business

Is it easy to do business with you?

A year or so ago, I pulled into a local car wash for a quick cleaning. I pulled a little further than I was supposed to as one of the workers annoyingly waived me back. Nice. I moved back to the unobvious starting position and waited. Don't customers just love waiting? Isn't that what retailers strive for? After all, we love to wait. Barriers. Anyway, there I sit in my car, waiting. I check email, play a letter in Words with Friends, and check email again. Look around – no one. I actually sat there for a good 5-7 minutes, which is forever in this kind of situation, and no one came by. No one said, "We'll be right with you, or "Sorry for the delay." No one even looked in my direction. In fact, other than the guy who waived me back in the beginning, I didn't see anyone who worked there. So, all the marketing, branding, location costs – all of it spent to get me and everyone else to come by – was wasted in my case. I left. Plus I told people. Lots of them. So do you. So do your customers and "would be" customers. Believe it or not, I actually went back, reluctantly, a few months later. It was out of pure convenience – right place and time. I pulled up – to the right spot this time. A worker walked toward my car (looking good…) and continued walking right by. No look, no comment, no nothing. Not again! But, eventually someone did come by and I went through the car wash. Clean car, but still lousy service.

Difficult to do business with. Barriers. Makes NO sense to me.

How about you? Is your team making it easy to work with? Do they greet people right away, with a smile and an attitude that suggests they might even want to like you and help you? Do you make people wait and if you do, because sometimes you must, how do you make it less painful or more efficient for the customer?

Is your building inviting? Is the parking the best it can be? Do you have the eternal phone tree for those of us calling in or a real person available to talk to another real person? Do you learn people's names and use them, appropriately? If you have restrooms, are they CLEAN? Is your web site interesting, engaging and easy to navigate?

What about you as a person? Are you easy to do business with? Are you easy to talk to? Does your demeanor invite people in or does it put out a sign saying "Danger: Thin Ice".

With all the customer service gimmicks, tricks and ideas, my #1 recommendation is this: Be easy to do business with. Be easy to talk to. Be fun. Be interesting. Be engaged.

People tend to take the path of least resistance. Think about it. Learn from it. Customer service success will become much easier when you do.

...a wealth of information creates a poverty of attention...

- Herbert A. Simon

Time Out 28
Fathead

"Howya doing, fathead?" This was a frequent greeting I would hear from my neighbor as he addressed my son Mitchell when he was a little toddler. Yep – fathead! But somehow it was okay, even funny – he just used it as a term of endearment and a creative and catchy way to engage with Mitch. But a CD I heard just recently showed me that real fatheads are everywhere, sometimes even in my own mirror!

This recording started out by citing that nearly 66% of our nation is considered to be overweight and roughly 33% is considered clinically obese. He went on to make the comparison to our minds – the constant overfeeding of our minds – some good, some not, but always lots of it! And how it can lead to what he referred to as the "fathead" – too much insignificant stuff clouding out the things that matter most. Infobesity.

Physical weight challenges are often blamed on the over availability of processed foods (it's too convenient and easy); yet, none of the food we eat just finds its way down our throat – it always has a willing assistant. Same goes for our brains – the information, though sometimes more subtle, is still *given* access by the owner – us! While there's certainly input we cannot avoid, the overwhelming majority of information clouding our brains is also welcomed in by that same willing assistant.

How do we get rid of this fathead syndrome?

- First, know that it matters. Know that what we put in comes out – consistency in yields consistency out – whether good or bad.

- Also, we can choose environments and pathways that limit negative exposure. No disrespect to the news, but most of it requires some real searching to find the feel good stuff. So perhaps some vetting may be in order.

- How about something proactive? Don't just block out the bad stuff, put in the good stuff. Get around people whose thinking stretches you to be better. Get around good friends, mentors, teachers, coaches. Find people with conversations that elevate your thinking. You don't even have to know them personally – John Maxwell will gladly provide one to one influence through a $20 book. Heck, read it 10 times and its cost comes down to $2 per reading!

If we're going to have the fat head, let's fatten it up with the good stuff!

You don't stop having fun because you get old; you get old because you stop having fun.

- Anonymous

Time Out 29
Find Your Fun

A few weeks ago my wife ran the Warrior Dash in the Poconos. Warrior Dash is the world's largest obstacle race series, held on the most rugged terrain in more than 50 locations across the globe. Participants earn their Warrior helmet by tackling a fierce 3-4 mile course and 12 extreme obstacles. After conquering the Battleground, Warriors celebrate with turkey legs, beer steins and live music at a post-race party in a league of its own. Amy finished by crawling in 2 feet of pure mud– forced on hands and knees because of barbed wire under which you must crawl. You cannot come out without being completely covered in mud. And she was.

It's likely many of you reading this have finished a mud run like the Warrior Dash. And I congratulate you. But very few, I suspect, share Amy's perspective. She hates to be cold, wet and dirty. She also hates to run. She does love FUN, though, and, for her, FUN trumps all.

How important is fun? What value does fun bring to your work and home environment? How much do you strive to bring fun in your daily experiences?

Rather than constantly striving for productivity, efficiency, respect and leadership, perhaps by focusing on a little more fun and engagement, all those other things will follow. The "best" places to work are usually the most fun places to work.

When we're relaxed, appreciated and smiling – having fun – we tend to be far more engaged. Engaged employees, engaged teens, engaged spouses, engaged membership, and engaged church goers are the most informed, contributing and joyful. Fun is one of the most important catalysts for engaging those around us.

By the way, I thought it would be fun to have Amy's Warrior Dash photo for this article. Amy didn't.

Go find your fun.

"The future will depend on what we do in the present."
- Mahatma Gandhi

Time Out 30
How not to Run a Marathon

My father has competed in over 69 marathons, all in a span of less than 20 years! By the time I was 16, he'd run over 80% of those races, and I approached him to train me to run the Philadelphia marathon. I figured it would be a good idea to train with someone who knew what he was doing before I actually attempted to run one. I also kind of figured I really didn't fully qualify as his son until I ran one. But my goal was one. Just one. Because I had good motivation and excellent training, it only took one attempt – goal achieved. I'm 47 now and haven't run one since. Not thinking of it either.

Here's the ironic part. Despite his obvious acumen in marathon running, my dad didn't actually set the bar high in terms of proper training for his first marathon. I just learned recently a little about that first race. Here's how not to train for a marathon... He ran long distances (15+ miles) daily up to the actual day of the marathon. Wrong. He ran with two different shoes! He liked them both and couldn't decide! Way wrong! He turned his ankle several days before and ran anyway, without proper medical attention. Dangerously wrong! He wrapped his own ace bandage and moved it to his thigh when that was hurting along the way. As it was eventually just dangling from his leg, he ripped it off entirely because it looked bad! Wrong.

I don't even remember if he actually finished that race, but I do know that he eventually figured out how to train properly as he went on to finish a total of 66 marathons.

Here's my transition into business application…The average manager gets into their first management role at the age of 27. Yet the average manager does not receive any formal training until the age of 42. Are you seeing an issue here? Why do most people get promoted into management? They performed well, were really smart and hung around a while – great prerequisite for managing, developing and guiding others, right? Wrong. Jim Clifton (CEO of Gallup), in his recent book, *The Coming Jobs War* cited that America has an epidemic of disengaged employees in its workforce today – far more than any time measured in the past. Poor management is one of the major culprits.

Could your manager use a dose of *How to Win Friends and Influence People*? People skills are far overlooked, considered far too simplistic, yet are the very skills that glue the relationships of a team together – for the benefit of all. There's certainly more to management training, but that would be a good start – before the manager starts!

Success consists of going from failure to failure without a loss of enthusiasm.

- Winston Churchill

Time Out 31
Life Lessons from Peter Pan

It was another family night at the Greene household, and this was Madi's night to decide what we would do. Would it be games, the fire pit, reading and a puzzle or perhaps another movie? Her pick – a classic: *Peter Pan*. Excellent! One of my favorite Disney films. As we were watching, I realized Peter's a pretty smart kid. He knows some stuff about life.

So, here's my take on some key life lessons from Peter Pan...

First, Peter said that in order to fly you need to think happy thoughts. The Bible fully supports this in Philippians 4:8, "Finally, brothers and sisters, whatever is true, whatever is noble, whatever is right, whatever is pure, whatever is lovely, whatever is admirable--if anything is excellent or praiseworthy--think about such things." This scripture doesn't reference flying, as we would define it, but we could make the argument that flying is a great metaphor for our overall success in life. So, think happy thoughts.

Second, Peter taught us to always keep our word. In fact, in the final fight scene with Captain Hook, Peter is goaded into committing to fight *without flying*, much to Wendy's chagrin. In fact, when she encouraged Peter with "Fly, Peter! Fly!" Peter responded by saying, "No! I gave my word!" If all of us kept our word, no matter what, much like Peter did, things might look a little better everywhere. Always keep your word.

Third, have fun. Everything Peter did was about having fun. There are certainly times for seriousness, but wow, we often take that perspective much too far. Maybe we should follow a little more of Peter Pan's mentality in life and lighten up a bit, and enjoy the ride. Have fun.

Last, he taught us to love our mother. After all, Peter risked a lot to have a mother for him and the Lost Boys. And in the end, despite the fact that he chose not to grow up, he did not begrudge Wendy and her brothers or the Lost Boys from going home to be with their mother. Because he knew how much it mattered to them. Love your mom. And dad, too!

There you have it. Four key life lessons from Peter Pan:

1. Think happy thoughts
2. Keep your word
3. Have fun
4. Love your mother

The two most powerful warriors
are patience and time.

- Leo Tolstoy

Time Out 32
No Parachute

Question for you: If you were offered $1,000,000 to jump out of an airplane without a parachute, would you do it? Most of us would answer this question with a resounding "no". After all, what's $1,000,000 to us if we're dead! And that might even be the right answer. But, as is usually the case, there's more to it.

Fact is, you don't have enough information to make an educated decision.

We often make decisions or draw conclusions without all the necessary details. Many of us are naturally wired to make quick decisions and that can sometimes come in very handy. But in the case above, that lack of patience – less questioning and more doing – might have cost us a bundle.

We cannot lead people correctly if we don't know what matters to them. We cannot sell effectively if we don't understand what our prospects want and why they want it. We cannot market if we don't know our audience and their interests.

We need to be interested, ask questions, listen, learn and ask more questions.

Let's see if we could have made a better decision about that

$1,000,000 proposal… Here are a few more questions that might have helped. What kind of plane are we jumping out of? Is it in the air when we jump? How fast is it going when we jump? Do I have full use of my arms and legs when I jump (just thought of that one!)?

If you are healthy, and the plane is a single engine Cessna, on the ground and sitting still, might that have changed your answer? Definitely!

When the answers are really important, be sure you know enough about the question before *jumping* to conclusions. (Sorry. Couldn't help myself.)

Your life does not get better by chance; it gets better by change.

- Jim Rohn

Time Out 33
Are You a River Person or a Lake Person?

My family would be the first to tell you that I love to rearrange our rooms – I love the change. And even after making the changes I'll sometimes just stop in the "new" room and look around a bit, appreciating and enjoying. Simple, I know, but that's me. It's also because I know that within a few weeks, and sometimes just a few days, the "newness" of the change won't be new anymore. Do you relate?

Lake water stands pretty still, unmoving and unchanging. Though the view can be remarkable, it will eventually grow a little old, as it's always the same – predictable, yes, and eventually a little boring. As beautiful as any view is, over time, you get to the point of not even noticing. Just like the room I just rearranged!

In contrast to the lake is the river. The river is always moving – headed somewhere, with purpose, without delay, relentless to get there. It's always changing; it's dynamic and exciting, even exhilarating at times. Its unpredictability can be unnerving and even dangerous, yet that's precisely what makes it so appealing.

So which are you? I suggest being a river person. Keep life exciting, challenging and even daring at times. Work to make yourself better. A better you provides a better product for those around you – your spouse, your kids, your teammates, your co-workers, your clients, even your dog!

Learn to love change, embrace it, and even lead it – within you and around you.

Be a river person… Like Helen Keller said, "Life is a daring bold adventure, or it's nothing at all."

People don't care how much you know,
until they know how much you care.

- Theodore Roosevelt

Time Out 34
Baiters

Have you been there? You meet a friend or associate for coffee and as the conversation develops, you feel set up to talk about the other person. Their questions are not about learning more about you, but about opening the opportunity for them to talk about them!

Baiters…

Imagine someone asking you about your new year's resolutions, and, immediately upon your answer, they dive into their resolutions – often without being asked. Because that's what they were really interested in –theirs, not yours.

Imagine someone asking about your last vacation. What do they really want to talk about? You guessed it.

Imagine you just came back from surgery, or just being sick. The baiter will ask the right question, but with the wrong intent. Because they had surgery once too, and you're about to hear about it!

I get that we want to talk about ourselves. I get that we need and want to find points of connection. People who are doing that are more subtle in the baiting and often kind of half interested in the person's answers and half into their own perspective.

Others, though, the true baiters are into full-scale set up mode. They post ambiguous statements on Facebook or Twitter – designed to drive people to ask the questions that lead them to turn the attention to them. Check your Facebook feed. Look for posts like…*Feeling sad today* or *It's been a tough weekend* or *What a jerk!* Don't they leave a question on the table? These statements are the bait and our question is the bite we take, the bite they're looking for; then they have us on the hook. Find the bait on Facebook. You'll then see a bunch of fish on the comment thread.

I write this because I know that as much as this self-centered form of conversation rubs me the wrong way, I sometimes do it. If I have a hook hidden within my question, I'm about to bait them. Being more aware, though, I'll often ask the question before speaking it…*Is this about them or me?* And if the hook is there, I need to recognize it and pull it out of my question.

That might be the right question before the question – *Is this about them or me?*

Remember, happiness doesn't depend upon who you are or what you have; it depends solely upon what you think.

- Dale Carnegie

Time Out 35
Be Awesome

"When I'm sick, I stop being sick and be awesome instead." These are the famous words spoken like a winner by Barney of the TV Series, *How I Met Your Mother.*

As funny as this TV sitcom is, I'm not big on some of the content, and Barney's lifestyle is no exception. Yet the guy has a great attitude! Phenomenal. And these words epitomize that attitude. The more I read them, the more I love them. "When I'm sick, I stop being sick and be awesome instead." Love that! Attitude in action!

Recently a friend was diagnosed with strep throat a day after we sat beside each other on a two hour flight. She's doing great now, thankfully, and was kind enough to reach out to me immediately after seeing her doctor – worried for me. My response was a little like Barney's but far less poetic. And the results matched my words. Healthy.

You see, my words elicit a cosmic response in the universe that naturally protects me from any and all germs. Doubt it. Yet, my words have been pretty good predictors of my experiences. And I'm not sick much, and certainly not for long. Haven't had the flu in...don't really remember. And no flu shots either. Not for 15 years. Is it really my words?

Naturally our words cannot deflect the harsh realities of sickness, disease and other challenges that may venture upon us. But I truly believe that our words, which start in our mind, often do influence the circumstances we encounter, and absolutely influence how we handle what comes our way.

Here's what the Mayo Clinic Staff has to say about the possible effects of a positive mental attitude (which I believe is best demonstrated by our words):

- Increased life span
- Lower rates of depression
- Lower levels of distress
- Greater resistance to the common cold
- Better psychological and physical well-being
- Reduced risk of death from cardiovascular disease
- Better coping skills during hardships and times of stress

And here are just a few things the Bible has to say about the power of our words:

- But what comes out of the mouth proceeds from the heart, and this defiles a person. (Matthew 15:18)
- There is one whose rash words are like sword thrusts, but the tongue of the wise brings healing. (Proverbs 12:18)
- A cheerful heart is good medicine, but a crushed spirit dries up the bones. (Proverbs 17:22)

All the way from Barney to Scripture! Nice.

Courage is what it takes to stand up and speak. Courage is also what it takes to sit down and listen.

- Winston Churchill

Time Out 36
Bumble Ballism

Do you remember the bumble ball?

It's is a life saver to parents and a blast for the little kids! I remember watching our daughter at 2 years old playing with one – it was so much fun to see her excitement at the constant, unpredictable, and exciting nature of this cool toy. Of course, seeing a dog or cat with it can be just as interesting! Love the bumble ball!

For a toy, it's great. For a lifestyle, not so much.

Years ago I observed a person who always appeared excited, enthusiastic, uninhibited and directionless. He was not afraid to take on challenges, embrace change and speak words of positive empowerment. The problem was that he had no clear direction. He was heading nowhere in particular, but with a positive attitude and constant movement. And he was the last one to recognize it. His enthusiasm and action led him to believe he had passion with purpose. He did have the passion, but not the clear purpose.

Here is some of what I observe about the bumble ball mentality:

1. Change is constant – not for the value of change, but because everything attracts attention

2. Excitement is evident – though not tied to any one purpose
3. Dependability is lacking due to the excitement of constant change
4. The "idea" of being positive is enough
5. More talking, less listening
6. Nothing is predictable – except unpredictability

Fortunately, in this case of bumble ballism, purpose was eventually married to passion and the dream realized. The bumble ball became a bowling ball. Strike!

Outstanding leaders go out of their way to boost the self-esteem of their personnel. If people believe in themselves, it's amazing what they can accomplish.

- Sam Walton

Time Out 37
Buy In

My wife is a busy woman. She's the type of person who will build daily to do lists, much like many of us. For me those lists are separated into compartments called days – Monday, Tuesday, Wednesday… And those points of separation work well for me. On Monday, I'm not thinking about Tuesday or Wednesday – most of the time. For Amy, her to do lists, though written by day, work more like a river – all flowing together. When she's working on Monday's list, she has a "tab" open for Tuesday, Wednesday, and even one or two things from next month's list! Needless to say, to me, this is a very stressful way to mentally manage tasks and priorities, but Amy says it's just how she is wired. And, while we can all change, I agree with her. Plus, she's remarkably productive this way. And more, this article is not about that!

I've said all this to set up the lesson. Let's face it, in similar ways we are all likely very busy and often very stressed – endlessly trying to be better, do more, and accomplish more. Whether at home or in your career, lots of things are happening at once, all amidst your own personal priority focus.

Well, the other day for Amy was very much like what I described. Add in the additional Christmas preparation, planning and priorities. When Amy was in the kitchen, working through her list and thinking about all the open tabs in her mind, Mitchell came bounding down the stairs. He sees his mom, takes notice of the situation immediately, and says, "Mom, have you ever had one of those days when you woke up feeling like you're going to be incredibly productive?"

Amy replies, "I guess so, why?"

Mitchell says, "Well, that's how I feel today! So what do you need done?!"

Man, I love that type of observation, initiative and devotion!

The point. Amy has *buy in* from Mitchell. He doesn't just offer his help out of obligation, but out of a sincere interest to help, to serve and make a positive difference in her day. Now, in truth, I can't say he bounds down the stairs every day in the same way. But he did this time.

If we don't find our team, kids or even our spouse typically running to our side and offering to help, perhaps the buy in isn't there like it could and should be.

As leaders, we'll have far greater success when our team has bought into us – and that typically starts with our actions and attitudes. It's comes from how we treat them, how we respect, appreciate and value them. It comes from a sense of compassion – we care; a foundation of trust – we always do what we say we'll do; and a confidence of stability – we're there for them, always.

Take the time to proactively invest in the relationships that matter. It's far easier to lead a team that wants to win with you than one that has to win with you.

We are judged by what we finish, not what we start.

- Anonymous

Time Out 38
Calm Under Pressure

Have you ever had your hand caught in the door of a car when the door was shut? It hurts. A lot. I had such a joyful experience many years ago. While standing at the car, I had my hand in a really bad spot. As I stood there, she closed the door and instant pain shot through my fingers! And yes, the door was completely shut.

What would you do?

If you would have asked me that question, not having actually experienced this, I would have said, I'd scream…"Open the #$@! door!" And the other person would first freak out, then try to figure out what was wrong, and then finally actually open the door. Too much time.

What did I do?

I calmly, but pretty intensely said, "Please open the door." She opened it right away, and I was free. Thankfully, there's a little "give" in the door, so I managed to avoid anything broken – just pretty bruised. Can't say I'd react that way again, but I was pleased with my reaction that time.

Pressure. Difficulty. Adversity. How do we respond in these conditions?

It's said that the real character of a person is revealed when that person is faced with true adversity.

Check out the true life story of Louis Zamperini in the book and movie, *Unbroken*. It's a remarkable story of a former Olympian who survived in a raft for 47 days after his bomber was downed in WWII and was sent to a series of prisoner of war camps.

Or consider Kerri Strugg during the 1996 Summer Olympics. The US Women's Gymnastics team had never won the women's all-around Gold Medal. She needed to land a strong vault (her specialty) to seal the victory, but fell on her first attempt, wrenching her ankle in the process. As she limped to make her second, and final vault, she pushed forward – through the pain and pressure. She ran down the runway, vaulted perfectly and stuck the landing – standing on one foot! It turned out, she didn't need that last vault to win, but she didn't know it at the time. Pretty impressive. Yes! But even more impressive, she did it, knowing she would further damage her ankle and clearly be unable to perform in the individual rounds.

Calm under pressure. Another key to success in business, athletics and life.

None of us is as good as all of us.

- Ray Croc

Time Out 39
Carrying Buckets

Are you a leader, manager, supervisor, sales person, volunteer, or parent? If you are, keep reading…

How many buckets do you carry every day? Buckets are the actions you take to do your "job". My guess is that it's a lot! Maybe too many buckets. And, then again, maybe many of those buckets aren't even yours. That's right, we often carry other people's buckets too. Isn't that just a bummer?

The best illustration I can think of is from a parenting perspective because, in my humble opinion, this is where parenting often goes really wrong. When I think back on my own life, how many times did I just do the thing I asked my kids to do? And why? Because it was easier, quicker, and frankly, I was better! But, wow, those buckets were sure heavy at times. And what happens when we are tired and frustrated and carrying heavy buckets? Yep. Stuff spills!

Here's the real fallout when you carry your kids' buckets, or from a business perspective, when you carry your team's buckets. You teach them they're not worthy. You teach them you'll do it better. You teach them not to try. You teach them that you don't trust them. You teach them to eventually carry their team's (or kids') buckets. You teach them impatience.

You teach them to limit their productivity to what they can do, rather than what the team can do. You teach them short term thinking, which can be long term costly – financially, relationally, emotionally.

The buckets are getting pretty heavy aren't they?

It's time to put some down, and let others do what is expected of them. Let the right people carry the right buckets. Focus on your own buckets – one of which is to TEACH others how to CARRY THEIR OWN BUCKETS! Teaching takes time. It's a heavy bucket, and it's filled with a powerful tool – equipping.

Carry that equipping bucket any time you want to do something for someone else who really should be doing it for themselves. Equip by teaching, demonstrating, and, ultimately, handing it over.

Think about the buckets you pick up this week. Should you really be carrying them? If not…put them down or grab the equipping bucket!

The power of our beliefs can work in either direction to become life affirming or life denying.

- Gregg Braden

Time Out 40
Defining Moments

I'm a pretty physical guy. I love to be in shape, move fast, run far, lift big (for a little guy), and of course, I love mud runs – especially the challenging ones. I also like keeping up with my son on the tennis court – for now. It wasn't always that way. Yeah, I've always been in decent shape, but mostly from good genes. Until, what I believe was a very subtle, but highly influential moment in my young life.

I was probably 12 at the time. My dad, then in his mid 40's and likely on the tail end of his wimpy lifetime achievement of running 66 marathons, had a resting heart rate of 46. That's right – 40 freakin' 6! Did I mention the marathons? What a nut. But a nut I respected. You don't get a resting heart rate of 46 by being in lousy shape, unless it's headed south fast, and you catch it on the way down! I remember around that time going to the doctor and finding out my resting heart rate was 80. 80! I don't really know how much it matters, but I've always believed a low resting heart rate is one sign of excellent conditioning. Unless it's zero. So 80 made me feel like a sickly little kid compared to my dad. Quite honestly, I've been chasing that 46 ever since. I don't know how conscious I've been of it, but it's always been a subtle inspiration to me. Silly as it sounds, I actually check my rate often – never quite hitting that elusive 46. Big picture – it's always been a subtle push that's led me to a much higher level of fitness and energy that I might not otherwise be experiencing.

Most of the change we see – both positive and negative – I believe comes through small, slow and consistent influences. As a coach, trainer and speaker, my confidence has been built slowly and surely around the influence of my wife, personal mentors, books, audios, and my faith in God.

And certainly many of us have experienced life changing, defining moments in other, much more difficult and challenging ways. We've all had a mix, but don't disregard the little stuff. Sometimes it goes deeper than we think.

What are your defining moments?

You're likely wondering, so I just checked – 49! Not Dad, but not bad.

All leadership is influence,
nothing more, nothing less.

- John Maxwell

Time Out 41
Your Top 5

Years ago, my friend and mentor told me that my income would be the average of the top 5 influencers in my life. Take the top 5 most influential people in my life, whether through direct or indirect (an author or speaker) relationship, add up their incomes, divide by 5, and that should be my income. Well, I could never quantify that for obvious reasons, but the idea has stuck with me to this day.

I've thought more about that statement and agree with it in concept. It stands to reason that if these are the top 5 influencers in my life, then I would tend to think and act somewhat consistently with them, thereby gaining similar outcomes, and thus financial results.

Let's go further. Income is nice, yes. But, what other things are really important, and how can we apply this principle of influence to help us in a similar manner?

For example, if you want to be a better father, check the top 5 influential father figures in your life. Who are they? Perhaps one of them is your father. In truth, don't most of us learn about marriage and family through our parents – whether good or bad? Who else? Perhaps a neighbor or uncle or even a coach or pastor. Let's go even deeper, what father figures have influenced you through the television? If you grew up when

I did, it was Mike Brady, Archie Bunker, Bill Cosby and Al Bundy. Not judging here…but who would you want your son influenced by most?

Think about it. We tend to behave on the basis of our paradigms – the perspective from which we view life. And we try to change those behaviors, often with the same paradigm. The easier way is to change our paradigm, which will lead to a change in behavior. Our perspective or paradigm is best changed by changing the way we think, which is most influenced by those around us – back to our top 5 influencers.

So here's the challenge: Where are you looking to improve? What is important to you? Your career, your marriage, your parenting, your health, your finances, your leadership? Take out a sheet of paper and list your top 5 influencers in those areas. Be honest – by thinking about who is getting into your head daily and how they do it. While many get there though direct influence, so much comes from indirect means – books, music, TV, movies, etc. Write out the list. Then determine if the thinking of those influencers matches what you want. If it does, keep it up; if it doesn't, change the source.

It's really as simple as that. Find the 5 people you'd like to influence you – in whatever matters – and get around them as often as possible, through whatever means is available. Today's technology makes this easier than ever before.

Go ahead, write the list. And begin the change

Knowledge is power, but enthusiasm pulls the switch.

- Ivern Ball

Time Out 42

Don't Wait For All the Lights to Turn Green

From our home to the highway on-ramp there are approximately 12 traffic lights. If I waited for *all* those lights to turn green before trekking out on a journey, how long would it be before I left my home? Would I ever leave? Not likely.

Yet, isn't that how many of us think when facing a major decision, a major change, doing something we fear, or something we want to avoid. Perhaps it's a challenging client call, sales opportunity, or perhaps a difficult call to a loved one. Maybe it's the new exercise plan we read about a few months back but haven't started, or maybe a habit we need to kick (like not exercising). Maybe you need to call that client about their poor payment history. Or you need to call that tenured employee into your office and finally hold them accountable for their poor attitude and its effect on the team.

Fact is, most of our life is a revolving door of these situations – and learning to address them in a timely, appropriate and effective manner is a representation of our maturity and growth. It's our willingness to move and adjust as we learn that makes us who we are. Whether all the lights are green or not, we go; adjust to each light as we encounter it, and continue on – growing and learning in the process.

Remember that procrastination is the assassination of motivation. Just go! And remember what Les Brown says, "Leap and the net will appear."

A happy family is but an earlier Heaven.

- George Bernard Shaw

Time Out 43

Are You Working IN Your Relationships or ON Your Relationships?

Have you read the best seller by Michael Gerber, *E-Myth*? You may remember the big question "Are you working IN your business or ON your business?" The truth is that most business owners spend far too much time doing their business, rather than investing time working on their business – strategy, planning, training, recruiting, systems improvements, etc.

All that said, it occurred to me that this similar principle applies to our relationships as well. Parenting, marriage, friendships, and even client relationships can, and often do, become very reactive – simply doing the relationship, responding to requests, paying household bills, being "side by side" with the TV on, working two separate careers, often passing in the night. Nothing innately wrong with these things, but I'd like to suggest investing more time ON the relationship – not just working IN it.

For clients this may involve a client loyalty plan – finding ways to proactively serve and build value in the relationship. These are the things you do for them when they don't necessarily need anything – a client appreciation event, a lunch get-together, an article of personal interest to them, connecting them to people you know and believe they would appreciate knowing.

For marriage and parenting, it may be creative date nights – with your spouse, and yes, even with your kids. Imagine taking your daughter out to lunch or a movie, just because. How about reading and learning from others through books, videos, church or other events? How about a family night, where each kid and adult gets a turn at choosing what to do as a family on certain nights? How about hiking? Anything to promote meaningful conversation, laughter, or any positive connection, certainly pays huge short and long term dividends.

I've read that fathers spend minutes a day at best communicating positively with their kids. I don't know if that's true, but I can see how it happens. Let's go back to Covey's story of the rocks in the jar, identify the rocks and become deliberate about putting those rocks in our jar first. I'm in.

I like to listen. I have learned a great deal from listening carefully. Most people never listen.

- Ernest Hemingway

Time Out 44
Listening Makes You Smarter

"You're not listening to me!" – One of the worst, yet most valuable sales lessons I've ever experienced. I was in a sales call when the prospect made this very accurate assessment of me. He was absolutely right as I spent most of my time thinking of what to ask and how to stay on track, missing all the cues he was giving me – all the education I had to learn from what he was saying. So worried I would miss something important in the sales process, I missed the most important part – what mattered to him!

I've heard it said that listening makes you smarter. Does listening really affect IQ? Not likely; but then again, what difference does IQ have on our ability to develop and grow relationships? In this sense, "smarter" is about listening to the point of knowing what questions to ask – because people tell us! Learn all about this in Allan Pease's short, but powerful book called *Questions are the Answers*. Questions lead to answers that in turn develop into smarter, deeper, more relating questions. While hearing is passive, listening is the active part that happens after you have asked a question. This is where you apply their answers to your next questions. Want to get to know someone? Ask questions, listen, ask more, and listen more. Truly, most people will keep providing fuel for you to keep that conversation going, making you far more interesting and attractive than the passive listener.

According to Jim Rohn, "One of the greatest gifts you can give someone is the gift of attention." Very few would disagree with the value of truly giving someone your full attention. My wife often says, "People move to where they feel valued." Think about that. Your kids, your spouse, your friends, your co-workers, your prospects and your team – they all move to where they feel valued. Are they moving toward you?

A man only learns in two ways, one by reading, and the other by association with smarter people.

- Will Rogers

Time Out 45
Pigs Don't Know Pigs Stink!

A few days ago my wife mentioned this phrase that a wise friend of ours used to say: "Pigs don't know pigs stink." Wow! There is so much truth and learning in this one little statement, I had to write about it! And just so we're clear, in the context of my wife's comment, I'm pretty sure I was not the pig.

Regardless, the fact of the matter is true, and pigs really don't know it – they stink! My buddy would say this often when referencing negative people. His point was simple: If we are negative and hang out with negativity, we don't know the difference. This applies across the board. If I am in sales and in the bottom 20%, but hang out with the bottom 20%, I really don't know it. If I am constantly bashing my wife with my friends, and they do the same, none of us knows the difference. In either case, we are feeding each other by always relating – unfortunately in a negative way! That is not to say we don't really know the difference; it's just that our environment does not support an awareness to positively change. So we just keep on slopping along in the mud!

One of the most valuable life lessons I learned was nearly 20 years ago – and yes, it was from that same friend. He taught me the value of positive association, specifically through reading a little every day from something that would inspire positive change in me. Books about leadership, people skills, communication, marriage, kids and parenting, finances, sales, etc., became a consistent element of daily association. After about 30 days I began to notice that many people around me were more and more negative. What was really happening is that I was changing and noticing the difference. They were not more negative; I was more positive.

Keeping with the theme, the pig (me) cleaned up and began to notice the mud, dirt, and slime that was around me (not the people, the attitudes and perspective!).

What about you? Are your sales where you want them? If not, check the sty – is it full of sales people at your level and below? If your marriage is not the way you want it, check the sty – is it full of people who relate and even seem to thrive on similar issues, without ever solving them? If you don't like your health, check the sty – is it full of others who constantly struggle with weight, exercise, and general fitness? If we want to change anything, let's check the sty and find the people who reflect the change we want in ourselves.

It isn't what you have or who you are or where you are or what you are doing that makes you happy or unhappy. It is what you think about it.

- Dale Carnegie

Time Out 46
The Little Man

Some time ago I was walking past my laptop and noticed a consistent forming and reforming of 3 dimensional pipes on the screen. The screen saver was doing what it was programmed to do when not in use. Of course, once I sat down and went to work, it snapped right to attention.

Isn't that just how our brain works? We are always thinking, whether we're aware of it or not. And what may be really scary is what we are thinking when we are not thinking – our mental screen saver. I believe that what is on that screen saver is the key to where we are really headed, the future we have yet to realize. Are we not thinking about what we don't want, don't have, or fear? Are we not thinking about a recent argument with our spouse, or one we think we'll have in the next few minutes? Are we not thinking about the poor sales we're experiencing, the money we don't have, the shape we're not in, the promises and commitments we haven't kept? Remember, even when we're not thinking we are thinking – potentially hours upon hours each day!

Years ago we taught our kids why and how to guard their gates – mostly their eyes and ears. But this advice isn't just for kids – it's for all of us who care where we are going. Decide to filter what influences your thoughts, and thereby your screen saver. Just as the background music at a department store can set the music in our minds much of the day, our environment – aware of it or not – is always influencing what makes up our screen saver.

I remember hearing Earl Nightingale's classic recording from the 1950's, *The Strangest Secret.* He spoke of a great earth machine, with all its size, power and influence – being led by a tiny little man sitting way up on top. The machine really doesn't care; it just does what it is directed to do. Moving forward, be ever more deliberate about engaging that little man – to get that screen saver working for you.

Life is either a daring, bold adventure, or it is nothing at all.

- Helen Keller

Time Out 47
Why We Love Action Movies

By "we" I mean us guys.

I was meeting with a very wise client one early morning when something he said hit me like an epiphany. He was talking about a book he recently read by John Eldredge called *Wild at Heart.* In it Eldredge shares the secret to every little boy's soul. What he wants and dreams about is a battle to fight, an adventure to live, and a beauty to rescue. There's more, of course, but you can read about that later.

The epiphany relates back to the night before.

Our family was watching *Captain America: Winter Soldier.* When the credits were finally rolling, Amy said, "Wow, that was a lot of testosterone!" It was the next morning, when Jason shared his reading of Eldredge's book, which I had read many years prior, that it hit me. This is why I love action movies! If Eldredge is right, it's actually God's fault. He put that spirit within me as a little boy. And everyone knows that men are really just grown boys, at least most of us.

I want to fight a battle – for my wife, my kids, and myself. For me, it's usually in the form of a mud obstacle race or a challenging workout or even professional goal accomplishment.

I crave the adventure to live. Again, that occurs in the trails and obstacles of my beloved mud runs, but also occurs on the professional landscape – working through the daily challenges of workplace successes and failures. The beauty to win: well, I have her, yet I strive to win her again every day. That's the P in Amy's marriage secret – CPR: Compromise, Pursuit, and Respect.

So give me the battle to win, the adventure to live and the beauty to rescue – I love it. It invigorates me. The more I embrace these three deep inner desires, the more alive I am.

And if it takes an occasional *Captain America* movie to live it out every once in a while, so be it. Maybe there's a little more to it than testosterone. Maybe it's just how I'm wired. I'm cool with that, and so is Amy.

So, guys, do you have a battle to win? Are you choosing an adventure to live? And, most important, are you rescuing your beauty every day?

Let's put LIFE back in living!

Be the change you wish to see in the world.
- Mahatma Gandhi

Time Out 48
A Culture is a Consistent Set of Actions

I believe our "culture" (the attitude and actions within our environment) is often a clear reflection of ourselves. It's a mirror; what we put out comes back – eventually.

Has your company posted its values or culture list for everyone to see? Have you read it? Can you recite it? Most important, do you live it and does everyone else? Just like you, I've seen lots of posted statements about vision, mission, culture, values, success traits, etc. on countless office walls, web landing pages, and even bumper stickers. Woopdiddlydoo! What difference do they really make if they are not modeled – consistently? What power there is in consistency! I will even say that customers and employees often see these posted statements as disingenuous or even hypocritical – if they are not being consistently lived by the leaders. Now, from the perspective of that employee, he or she can "lead up" by living out those principles. That is the leaders' role – so who is the leader?

And is that leader consistently living out the culture they want to create and keep? Look around and what do you see? Do you see lots of drama, negativity, pessimism, blaming, and victim-mentality, or do you see personal responsibility, ownership, accountability, risk-taking, innovation, and integrity? What would you prefer? Define it, and then live it – all the time.

Remember this: a culture is a consistent set of actions. Check your actions – be sure they align with your values and that you live them consistently.

Usually the first problems you solve with the new paradigm are the ones that were unsolvable with the old paradigms.

- Joel A Barker

Time Out 49
Pike Syndrome

The pike is a large fish that survives by eating smaller fish. An experiment was conducted years ago where the pike was placed in a large fish tank. Then several smaller fish were introduced into the tank, but separated from the pike by keeping them within in a large, bottomless, glass jar. The jar was submerged to the bottom of the tank, closing them off completely from the pike. Of course, the pike didn't know this and immediately struck at the minnows. In fact, the pike hit the glass over and over until, frustrated and "conditioned", it settled at the bottom, right next to the minnows. After a while, the jar was lifted, and the minnows swam all around the pike and throughout the large tank. And yet, the pike remained motionless. Indeed, the pike never tried again and died in that tank with its main source of food and survival right in front of it!

Are we like that pike?

Do we have limiting beliefs that have conditioned our thinking, our actions and thus our results? Are we "too busy" to exercise, to sell more, to read, to even listen to our kids, our spouse, or our co-workers? Are we bad at remembering names? Are we living an average life, with average income, average cars, in an average home? Do we have average thinking?

While many second generation successes throw away the hard-earned rewards of their parents' efforts, many do not. Many in fact, continue in their parents' success – why? I think it's because they believe they can; it's the "condition" they know because it's what they grew up believing.

Steven Covey says, "If you want small changes in your life, work on your attitude. But if you want big and primary changes, work on your paradigms." The researchers were successful in changing the pike's paradigm towards its ability to eat the minnows and, consequently, condition the pike to starve itself.

We need to assess our paradigms, our "Pike Syndromes", and determine how we should view life rather than simply accepting it as we see it now. Change those paradigms by getting around those with the perspective you want.

If you want more time, more focus, and more energy – find those who seem to have it. Learn how they think; choose to be influenced by them, and you'll eventually gain their paradigm.

Eddie Murphy and Dan Aykroyd proved this in the classic 1983 movie *Trading Places*. Time to trade places – become what you want, not necessarily what you have.

The purpose of our lives is to add value to the people of this generation and those that follow.

- Buckminster Fuller

Time Out 50
Energy

We saw him walk into the lobby of the beautiful hotel in Waikiki. He didn't do anything in particular, didn't have an extravagant or flamboyant outfit or hairstyle. He wasn't loud or obnoxious so as to draw attention. And yet he did draw attention – everyone's attention. As soon as he walked in, there was "something" that was compelling about his presence. Who was he? Just a business leader, father, husband, and all around good guy. And yes, a millionaire. Those things were not apparent at this moment though. It was his presence, his energy. It took over the room and grabbed our focus.

Have you ever met someone who just "was someone" when they walked in the room? They didn't necessarily do anything unusual or special, but for some intuitive reason, you just knew they were "somebody", and so did everyone else.

Now, we are all "somebody", but few of us view ourselves that way. I don't mean in an arrogant, self-serving sort of way, but rather, a way that suggests inner confidence and ultimate self-assuredness. I can think of a few people who fit this description and one thing that seems to be apparent in all of these people is energy or presence. They exude energy, purpose, direction.

I remember reading in David Schwartz's book, *The Magic of Thinking Big*, that to gain confidence, we should consciously walk 25% faster – because it looks as if we know where we are going and we're excited to get there (why wouldn't we be, if we, being confident and purposeful, chose to go there in the first place?!). I believe we can increase our physical energy through good habits like eating, rest and exercise. But we can also create good energy (presence) through choice – simply by being purpose-driven in all we do – not necessarily goal driven, purpose-driven.

Next time you're at an event – business or pleasure, doesn't matter, look around and see if you can spot that person of unique presence. Take a "chance" and introduce yourself – you might be surprised how much can be learned in that moment. Perhaps at some point, if not already, you'll be that person for someone else.

Trying to be someone else is a waste of the person you are.

- Unknown

Time Out 51
3 Envelopes

The story goes that the new CEO was taking over and meeting with the exiting CEO about some final details. The former CEO said he had 3 sealed envelopes prepared, numbered and placed in the desk of the new CEO. Only upon any major mistakes as CEO was he to open them, and then in order. Well, after a few months, it happened – first big mistake! He went to the desk, pulled out the first envelope, opened it, and it said, "Blame me." So, he put it all on the decisions of the previous leadership, and everyone bought it.

About six months later, he made his second major mistake and again proceeded to the desk for wisdom. The second envelope read, "Blame the board," and he did. After all, much like the former CEOs policies, the existing board members were also inherited. This advice worked just as well.

Then, about a year later, he made his third major mistake. That last envelope was opened and provided the following masterful advice: "Prepare three envelopes!"

Perhaps if he didn't open that first envelope, he wouldn't have had the need to apply the wisdom of the third envelope! The blame game rarely works, and when it does, it really doesn't. Instead of blaming, denying or giving excuses – the latter of which may be the worst – it's time to lead. It's time to accept ownership, take responsibility and be accountable. Choose that path, and you'll feel better, grow faster, and ultimately gain the respect of those around you.

Here are three great answers to memorize and watch for: "Yes, sir!"; "No, sir!"; "No excuse, sir!"

If you don't like something, change it. If you can't change it, change your attitude. Don't complain.

- Maya Angelou

Time Out 52
A Walking Billboard

Have you ever waited on tables? Dealt with rude customers? Dealt with customers with no patience or empathy? Have you ever been tipped almost to the point of insult or even stiffed? Have you been on the other side? Have you been that customer? What does that speak of you? Regardless of the circumstances that may have influenced the poor experience, your actions are your billboard. They are on display for people to judge, right or wrong, and to make broad speculation – about what they think you represent.

My daughter waits on tables at a local restaurant part time – and we've heard a few of these stories. One in particular inspired this article. She waited on a large Christian group who were impatient and rude, and let's just say a little tight in the tipping department. The restaurant was clearly understaffed due to the late hour, and my daughter was openly distressed, yet the treatment she received was rash and inappropriate – not met with understanding and patience in any way. A lot more can be said about this experience that won't go into this writing. It just struck us that regardless of our faith, hers or the beliefs of the other staff that were serving that night, Christianity took a hit – not for its foundation, but for the billboard on display. This billboard, in my opinion, was inaccurate and unfair, but on display just the same. And, right or wrong, some will attribute the actions of those people to their understanding of Christianity. "…I remember meeting a group of Christians – impatient, rude and cheap…"

Most who are reading this know where I stand in my faith, which goes for my daughter as well. So please understand that writing this isn't easy, yet that's just the reason to write it.

Everything we do is a walking billboard for what others associate with us – our marriage, our company, our job, our country, and absolutely, our faith.

What's your billboard saying?

About the Author

Mike is the owner of IntegrityWorks Coaching – an integrity-driven training company focused on professional speaking and training in the areas of motivation, communication, performance, teamwork, relationships, leadership, sales development and sales management. Additional one on one coaching provides direct personal and professional development through sales, executive and life coaching.

For over 25 years, Mike has been an exceptional sales and business leader with proven experience in professional speaking, one on one coaching and development, sales planning and execution, and training and workshop facilitation, while building strong and lasting relationships with clients, associates and partners.

Mike and his wife Amy have been married for over 25 years – committed to an exciting relationship centered in their faith and what Amy calls CPR (compromise, pursuit, and respect). Mike and Amy have three children – their first three protégés in life and plan nearly everything around family.